A dog's-eye view of bird life.

The blue heron, an albatross, loons, and eagles are among the birds that Peter Parnall's famous dog seeks out, chases, and sometimes hides from in this playful picture-book guide to a variety of feathered folk.

Readers will remember this adventurous dog and his earlier preoccupation with bugs in Elizabeth Griffen's *A Dog's Book of Bugs,* illustrated by Peter Parnall.

Peter Parnall was born in Syracuse, New York and lives now with his wife and son in Maine. He is author and illustrator of many distinguished books, including *The Mountain* and *Alfalfa Hill,* and is the illustrator of two Caldecott Honor Books, *The Desert Is Theirs* and *Hawk, I'm Your Brother,* both with texts by Byrd Baylor.

A DOG'S BOOK OF BIRDS

A DOG'S BOOK OF BIRDS

by Peter Parnall

Charles Scribner's Sons • New York

1 3 5 7 9 11 13 15 17 19 MD/C 20 18 16 14 12 10 8 6 4 2
Library of Congress Cataloging in Publication Data
Parnall, Peter.
A dog's book of birds.
SUMMARY: Illustrates a dog's self-sought encounters with a variety of birds including a blue heron, albatross, loon, and eagle.
1. Birds — Pictorial works — Juvenile literature.   [1. Birds — Pictorial works] I. Title.
QL676.2.P37   598.2   77-7194   ISBN 0-684-15181-2

To Gus, Jeff, Charley, Ritzy, Max, Winston, Nitra, Finnigan,
Rufus, Luke, Mikey, and another Gus. Dogs.

This book
is for
curious,

adventurous,

and
seaworthy dogs...

who happen to like

birds.

Birds are everywhere.

They are in,

on,

above,

and under the water.

They are all around, all of the time.

Here's a bird moving slowly.

A Flamingo.

She strains
her food
out of the
mud,

and uses that mud to make a nest.

It looks like a
volcano.

Stilts?

No, Blue Herons.

They catch their food with VERY sharp beaks!

This bird swims.
Some call him a Snakebird,

but his real name
is Anhinga.

It takes a long time
to dry his wings.

She dives
for her dinner.

Pelican.

She catches fish in a pouch.   A TWO-GALLON pouch!

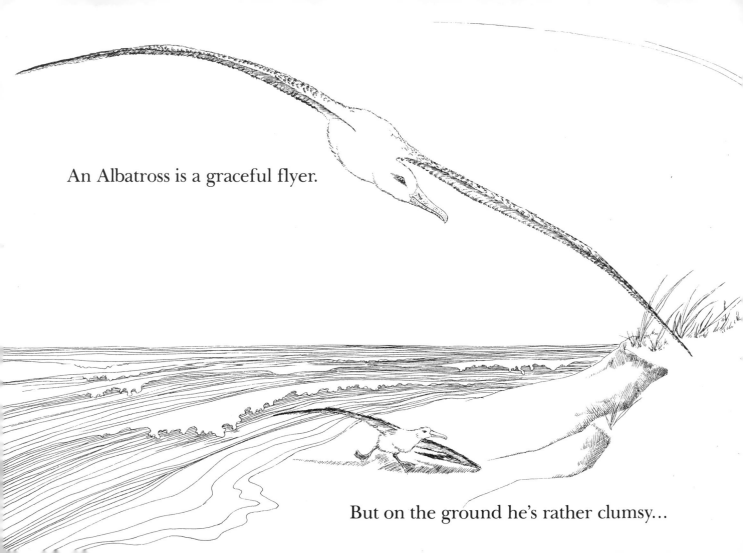

An Albatross is a graceful flyer.

But on the ground he's rather clumsy...

and sometimes does a
somersault when he lands.

What?
Dogs in the air?   No,

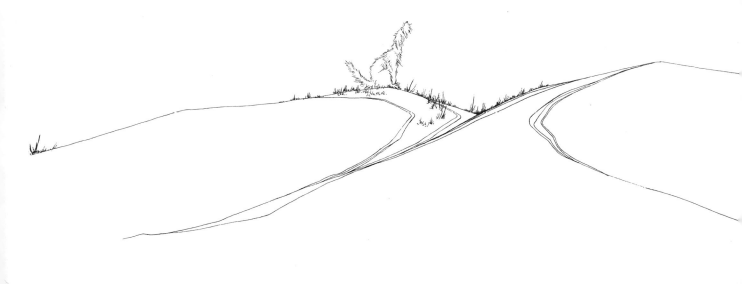

a family of Geese, flying in formation.
These are heading north (or maybe south).

Loons laugh,

Eagles scream…

and eat a lot of fish.

They build HUGE nests!
Some are more than ten feet deep.

Are they
dangerous?

No. Vultures eat only dead things.

They help keep the country clean.

Some Owls are
tiny.

The Elf Owl
is only six inches
tall.
He lives in
the desert.

The Snowy Owl is one of the largest.
He lives in the Arctic. (Most of the time.)

Hear that drumming in the woods?

A Grouse...

beating his wings VERY hard.
This is how he calls his friends.

Here's a bird that digs for worms.

A Woodcock.

He reaches for them   with his long beak.

The Red-winged
Blackbird.

She builds her nest in the reeds,
over the water and far away...

from creatures that creep...

and crawl...

and prey!

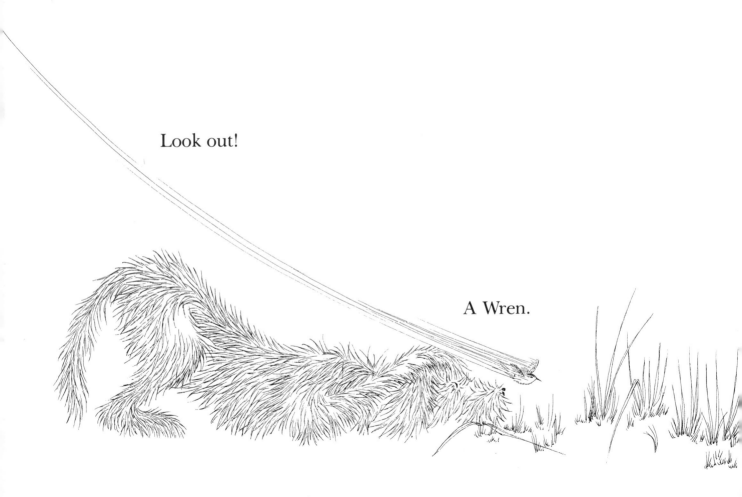

Look out!

A Wren.

Though small in size,
he
swoops…

and scolds…

and is afraid of no one.

The Crow is a rascal.

He makes a
lot of
noise…

and steals things.

He can even learn to talk.

A Roadrunner LOVES to run.

A very good bird!

He eats snakes,

scorpions,

spiders,

and is a friend to the...

Burrowing Owl,

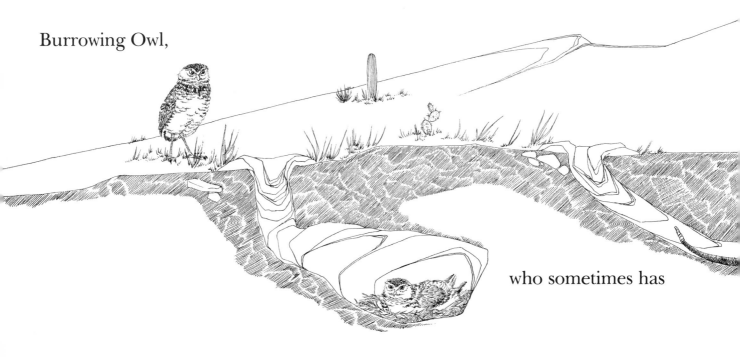

who sometimes has

unwelcome visitors.

To sleep he
borrows a burrow…

and so do we.